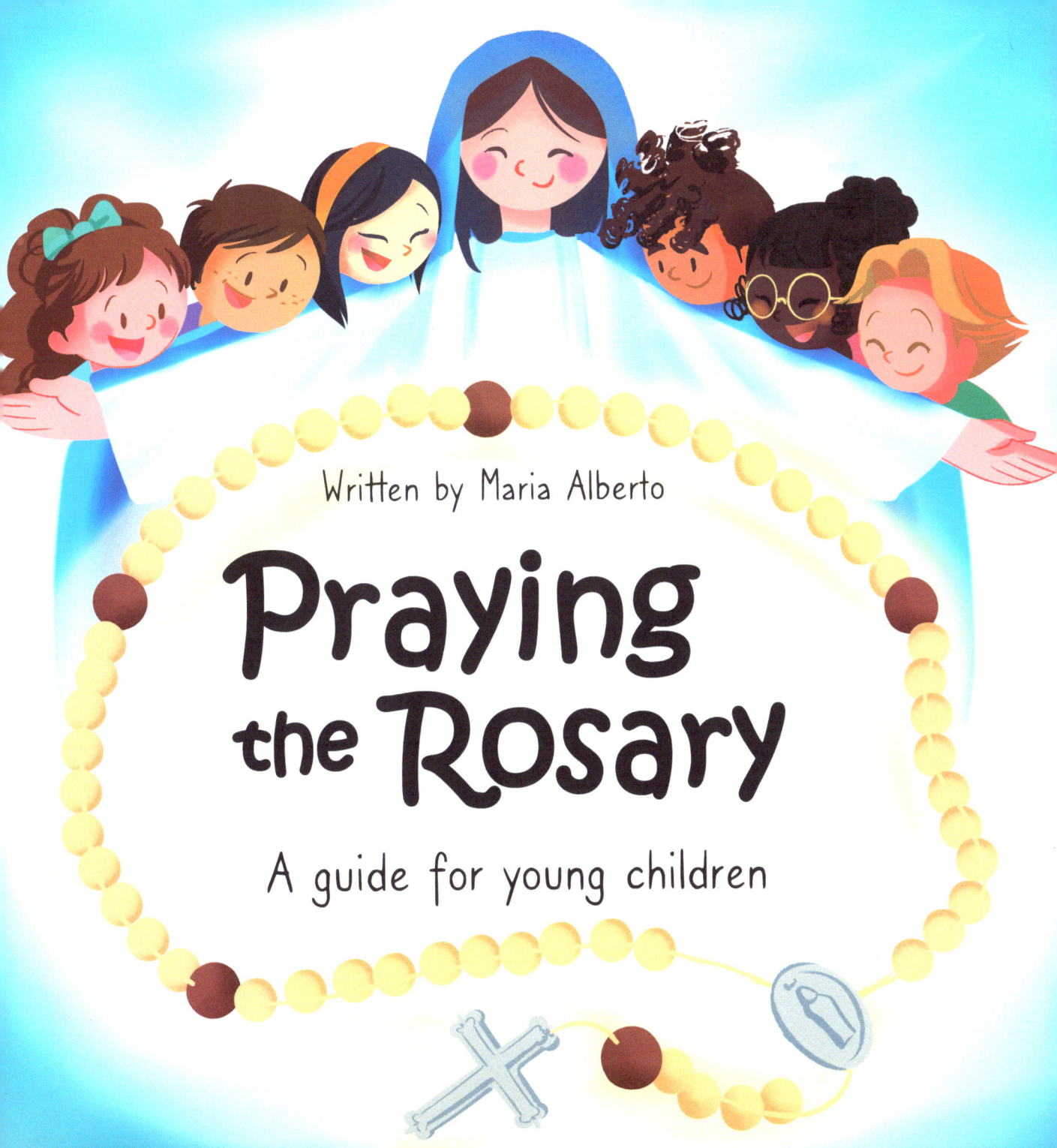

Written by Maria Alberto

Praying the Rosary

A guide for young children

© Maria Alberto 2025
All rights reserved. No part of this publication may be reproduced, stored in a retrieval system, or transmitted, in any form or by any means—electronic, mechanical, photocopying, recording, or otherwise—without the prior written permission of the copyright owner.

Dedication

For all little hearts learning to love Jesus, especially Julian and Adreana.

Ad Majorem Dei Gloriam

Before we start: why do we pray the Rosary?

The Rosary is a special way of praying and thinking about the life of Jesus. It is a gift shared with us by Mother Mary so that we can know more about God's love for us.

The Rosary Beads

The beads help us to keep track of what we have prayed. Touching them also helps us to stay focused.

Have a look at your set...

Does it have any special medals?

What else do you notice?

The Mysteries

In the Rosary, we think about important moments in the lives of Jesus and Mary. These moments are called *mysteries* because they are full of wonder and teach us about God's love.

For each mystery we pray:
1 Our Father
10 Hail Marys
1 Glory Be

Joyful Mysteries

We think about happy times in the lives of Jesus and Mary.

(Prayed on Mondays and Saturdays)

1. The Annunciation

The angel Gabriel appeared to Mary and asked her to be the Mother of God. Mary said "Yes!"

We pray that we can be brave like Mary and say yes to God's plan for our lives.

2. The Visitation

Mary was pregnant with Jesus.
She still travelled a long way to help her cousin
Elizabeth, who was also having a baby.

We pray that we always help others,
even when it's not easy for us.

3. The Nativity

Mary and Joseph went to Bethlehem but there was nowhere to stay. They had to rest in a stable with animals, and that's where Jesus was born.

We pray that we can welcome Jesus into our hearts.

4. The Presentation

Mary and Joseph took baby Jesus to the temple and offered him to God.

We pray for our Church and priests.

5. Finding Jesus in the Temple

At 12 years old, Jesus went to Jerusalem with His family. He went missing for 3 days, and His parents were so happy when they found Him safe in the temple.

We pray for the joy that comes from finding Jesus.

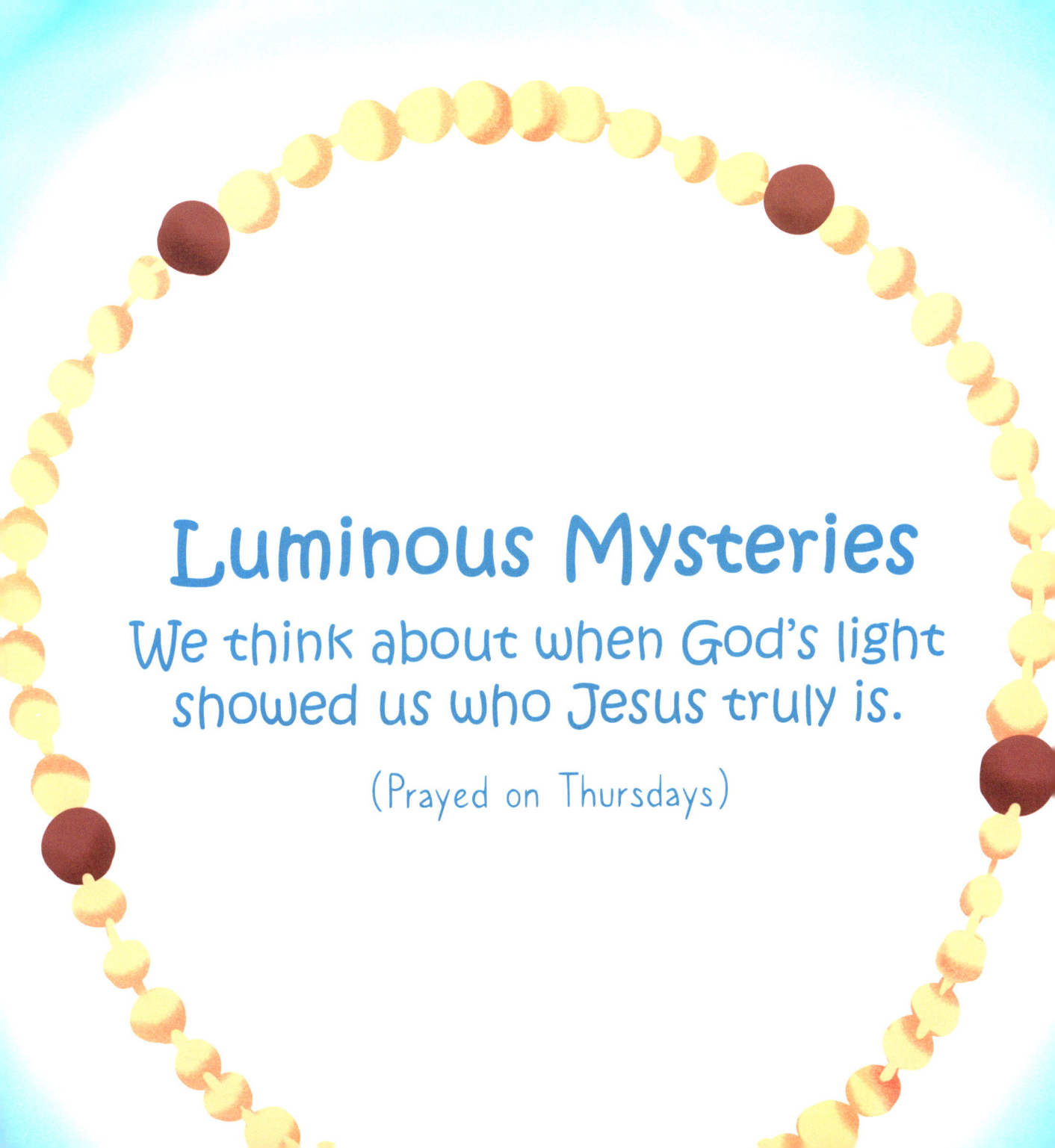

Luminous Mysteries

We think about when God's light showed us who Jesus truly is.

(Prayed on Thursdays)

1. The Baptism of Jesus

Jesus went to the River Jordan and was baptised by His cousin, John. When Jesus came out of the water, God spoke from Heaven and said: "This is my beloved Son".

We pray to know more about Jesus and what makes Him so special.

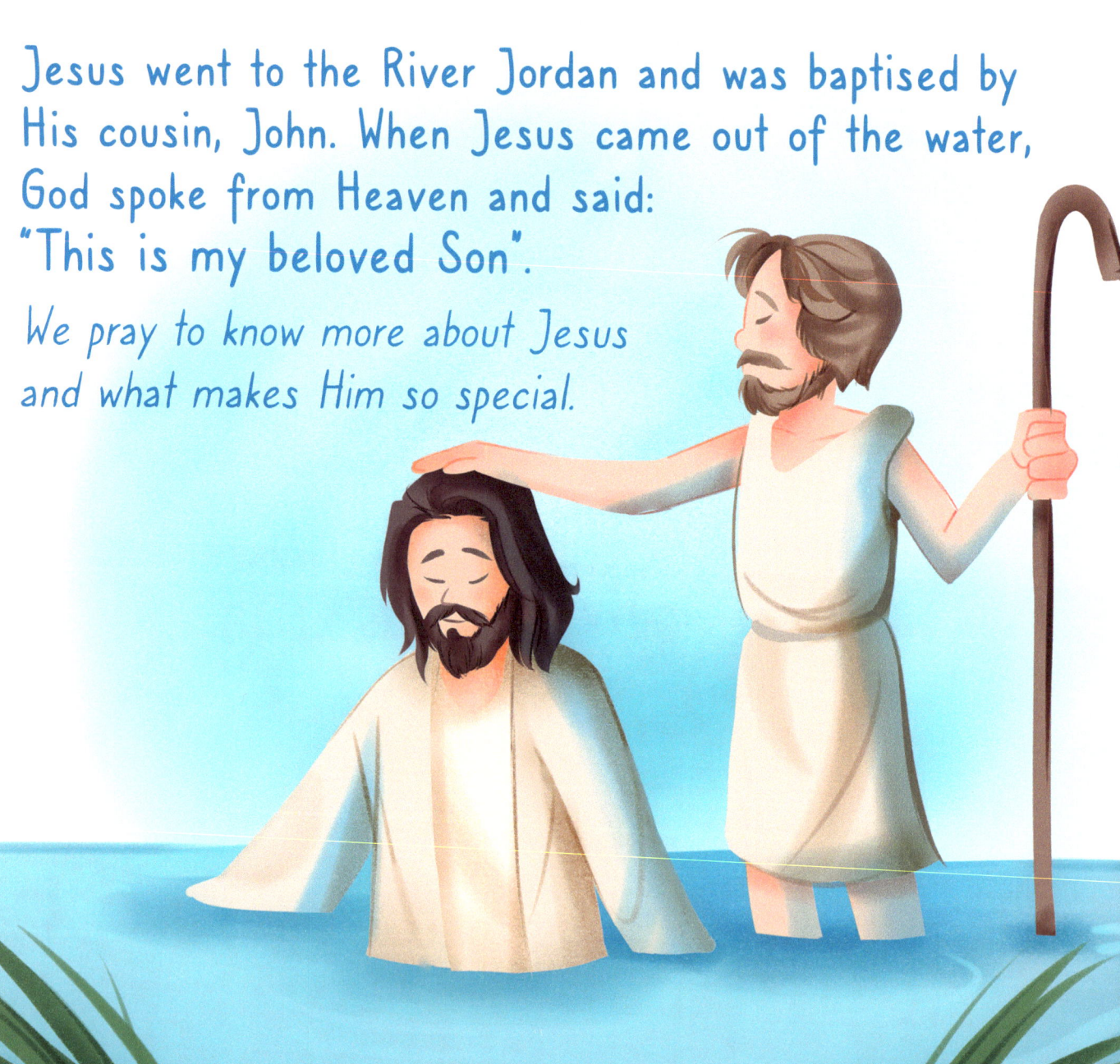

2. The Wedding at Cana

At a wedding, Mary asked Jesus to perform a miracle. Jesus did, and He turned water into wine.

Mary, please take our prayers to Jesus.

3. Jesus Proclaims the Kingdom of God

Jesus taught everyone about Heaven and how God wants us to live on earth.

We pray that we live the way Jesus tells us to, by loving God and loving each other.

4. The Transfiguration

On top of a mountain, Jesus showed His disciples that He is more than just a special person... He is the Son of God.

We pray that we show Jesus to others through love and kindness.

5. The Institution of the Eucharist

Jesus knew His time on earth was ending, so He chose to stay with us in blessed bread and wine.

We pray that we can love Jesus when He is 'hidden' in the Eucharist.

Sorrowful Mysteries

We think about some of the sad times in Jesus' life.

(Prayed on Tuesdays and Fridays)

1. Agony in the Garden

Jesus went to pray in the garden because He knew He was going to suffer. He felt scared, but He trusted in God's plan.

We pray for trust in God's plan for our lives because He knows what's best for us.

2. The Scourging at the Pillar

The soldiers took Jesus and, even though He had done nothing wrong, they hurt Him.

We pray for Jesus to be with us when we feel hurt.

3. The Crowning with Thorns

The soldiers put a prickly crown on Jesus to make fun of Him.

We pray that we do not stand by when people are hurt by others.

4. The Carrying of the Cross

Jesus was given a heavy cross to carry and, even though He was hurt, He agreed to do it.
We pray for Jesus to help us when we have to do hard things.

5. The Crucifixion

Jesus was nailed to the cross and died.
He did this for us so that we can be with God in Heaven.
We thank Jesus for loving us so much.

Glorious Mysteries

We think about how amazing God is!

(Prayed on Wednesdays and Sundays)

1. The Resurrection

Jesus rose from the dead, just as He had promised!
We thank Jesus for always doing what He says He will.

2. The Ascension

Jesus went to Heaven to make a place for us.
He promised that He would return.
We pray for hopeful hearts.

3. Descent of the Holy Spirit

Jesus promised us a helper, the Holy Spirit, who came down on the disciples in the form of fire.
We pray for the Holy Spirit to live in us.

4. The Assumption of Mary

Mother Mary is so special that God took her to Heaven, body and soul.
We pray that we can love Mary like God wants us to.

5. The Coronation of Mary

God crowned Mary as Queen of Heaven and Earth, honoring her humility and goodness.

Mother Mary, please pray for us.

Let us pray

O God,

As we think about the mysteries of the most Holy Rosary, help us to learn from them and receive what they promise. We ask this through Christ our Lord. Amen.

Tips for praying the Rosary with young children

1. Start with one Hail Mary for each mystery and build up.

2. Give your child a special set of Rosary beads to keep.

3. Help your child lead a mystery.

4. Pray the Rosary anywhere... in the garden or on a walk.

5. Create a family ritual like Friday night Rosary and movie.

A Note for the Grown Ups

The Christian family has long been described as the 'domestic church'. This means that our mission to build the Kingdom of God starts at home. Thankfully, we have a special gift to help us in our important work: the Holy Rosary. In fact, Saint Josemaria Escriva said:

"If you pray this every day with a spirit of faith and love, Our Lady will make sure she leads you far along her Son's path."

It is hoped that this book helps the young children in your life to connect with this powerful form of prayer and to love Jesus more deeply.

Ad Jesum per Mariam.

For further (free) resources, visit:
www.therosaryproject.net

www.ingramcontent.com/pod-product-compliance
Lightning Source LLC
Chambersburg PA
CBHW041459220426
43661CB00016B/1197